Ramiz D

The plight of Columbus after his travels

Science-popular essays

Baku-2022

Scientific editor and Preface: - Academician Ramiz Mammadov
Reviewer: - Doctor of Philosophy in Technical Nadir Achmedov
                   Doctor of Philosophy in Geography Shamil Azizov
Translator: - Hokume Hebibova
Computer operator: - Sinay Gasimova
Computer design: - Sevinj Akchurina
Ramiz Daniz. *"The plight of Columbus after his travels"*
                          - 108 p.   Baku – 2022

The Spanish monarchs cancelled monopoly of Columbus on the coasts of the New World when he was suppressing rebellion in the lands, he discovered. The Spanish officials cancelled the contract signed with the admiral on April 10, 1495 during his second travel (1493-1496). Some captains and navigators, who once were colleagues of Columbus, used this opportunity and began to organize expeditions towards the other side of the Atlantic Ocean as his rivals.

That decision resulted in losses for the creditors of Columbus too. Mostly his compatriots financed his travels. It is known that, the first travel of Columbus (1492-1493) was financed by Luis de Santángel - financial adviser and treasurer of the kingdom, who was close to the king Ferdinand, and Francesco Pinelli, who was known in Spain as Pinelo.

The French physician Jan Ferrell wrote that, the length of the Earth's outline was 39816 km and its radius was 6337 km. It means that, Toscanelli had made a mistake. According to his calculations, the length of the Earth's outline was 29000 km. I think that, Columbus had read at least part of **"Zij-i Ilkhani"** written by Nasiraddin Tusi before his travel.

The writer, researcher and publicist Ramiz Daniz was born in Baku in 1965. He graduated from secondary school in 1983. He has been a President grant holder since 2009 and he is a laureate of the *"Golden pen"* (2005) award. He is member of The Union of Azerbaijan Writers (1999) and Geography Society (2013).

He was winner of the international award instituted by the International Writers Union on 3 nominations in 2020 and Grand-Prix winner of the international award in 2021.

Preface - The plight of Columbus after his travels

The President's grant holder and laureate of the "Golden pen" award Ramiz Daniz (Gasimov) writes various literary and scientific works. His scientific works astonishes scientists of geography, astronomy and history of mathematics.

He has described obscurities of Columbus's first travel and very interesting facts concerning the unknown map used by him during the expedition in his work **"Christopher Columus, Nasiraddin Tusi and real discovery of America"**. R. Daniz has denied known information and mentioned that, Columbus knew the destination, route and term of his travel, but kept it secret. Of course, this is a serious judgement. Reasons why three expeditions sent by Portuguese to the western part of the Atlantic Ocean in order to find the forth continent failed have been explained in the work. The author has proved by indicating perspicacity of Spanish monarchs and disbelief of the king of Portugal that *"Mathematical Union"* of Lisbon had significant role in appropriation of those territories by Spaniards. Besides it, Ramiz Daniz has mentioned that, Columbus had used calculations of scientists of the East including Nasiraddin Tusi when he prepared his project.

"Enigmatic discovery of Brazil" concerns the problem, which make scientists of geographical discoveries to hesitate, and the author tries to prove that Brazil wasn't discovered by Pedro Cabral in 1500 by accident, it was discovered by Duarte Pereira in 1494 in accordance with secret agreement reached with the king of Portugal, but the result of that travel was kept secret for some reasons. In accordance with this work, Portuguese were able to conceal Spaniards by means of the Pope and became owners of today's Brazil according to Tordesillas treaty concluded in 1494. Though Portuguese were agree to own lands located at 100 liq west of Azores in 1493, in accordance with the result of the secret expedition of Duarte Pacheco, who visited American coasts after a year, they appropriated large territories by moving the demarcation line between Spain and Portugal for 270 liq towards the west.

The author has described scientific activities and achievements of the remarkable scientist N. Tusi, essence of most of his works known all over the world in his next

work *"The scientist passed ahead of centuries –
Nasiraddin Tusi"* and mentioned that, several works of
the scientist had been published by other authors as their
own works.

It is known that, Nasiraddin Tusi wrote masterpieces
in fields of astronomy, mathematics, geometry and
ethics, played a significant role in development of these
sciences and passed ahead of well-known scientists for
hundreds of years. The author has remembered scientific
works carried out by the most ancient scientists of
Greece, ancient Rome, Byzantine, Egypt and Muslim
scientists of the early middle ages, mentioned that, N.
Tusi had significant achievements in listed branches and
tried to emphasize Tusi's genius.

According to the book, the astronomical table *"Zij-i
Ilkhani"* prepared by Nasiraddin Tusi was used for
discovery of America. Ramiz Daniz mentioned it in the
book, which explains most issues concerning Tusi's
scientific activity and causing scientists of the world to
think. The scientist had described the prime meridian at
34^0 west of today's Greenwich Meridian (remote north-
western coast of Brazil) and this fact helped Columbus
when he passed the ocean.

Another interesting moment is the investigation of the real owner of the map made by the Turkish admiral Piri Reis in 1513, which has been analyzed in most science centers.

Though America was discovered 500 years ago, that discovery is still interesting for most experts as it is very enigmatic. Ramiz Gasimov could explain most details about discovery of America. This book includes answers of most questions, which were enigmatic during centuries.

Books full of rich historical facts and sensational information will be interesting for scientists all over the world and attract special attention. Discovery of America and Brazil is the most interesting part of the history of geographical discoveries and these books are significant source for deep investigation of mentioned theme.

Scientific works of Ramiz Daniz may be spread among scientists and ordinary readers interested in the history of geographical discoveries. Ramiz Daniz has found out new facts and so could destroy stereotypes concer-ning this field.

The author has proved following facts in his book **"The plight of Columbus after his travels"**: Vespucci travelled to America twice as a merchant, but not quadrice and 32-page letter, which brought him fame, is a copy of some lines of diaries of Pero Vaz de Caminha, Diego Chanca and Christopher Columbus.

Result of the research carried out by the author:

1. The author has found out that, Vespucci's correspondence with the king of Portugal Manuel I wasn't real.

2. The map made by Waldsemuller in 1507 was handed over by Vespucci.

3. Secret proposals of Vespucci as the navigation officer of Castile had a significant role in naming the forth continent America in books and maps prepared by most geographers and cartographer. It means that, he used his powers in order to name the continent, discovered by Columbus, "America".

4. In general, the author declared that, it is unjust to name the New World "America" and scientists all over the world have to make serious steps to correct this mistake.

The material including rich historical facts and some facts, which aren't noted in any scientific source, will certainly attract interest of the world's scientists and this discovery will have special significance. Very likely, the work will be discussed in Portugal, Spain and countries of the continent of America, the discovery of Brazil will be analyzed differently and some corrections will be made in the world's encyclopedia at the result of the objective decision.

In general, it should be noted that, all three works are great present of Azerbaijan to the geography, so owing to them remarkable and well-known universities and unions of geography will acknowledge that, the history of geographical discoveries is investigated in Azerbaijan, which have ancient roots and rich culture as well.

Ramiz Mammadov – Laureate of State Prize
Associate Member of the Academy of Science,
doctor of technical sciences, director of the Institute
of Geography of the Academy of Science

The world that seems from the window of Europe

People tried to discover unknown lands using primitive methods in order to appropriate new territories since ancient times and continued this work for centuries. Astronomers, geographers, cartographers, travelers, cosmographers, researchers and historians did their best for learning the Earth and carried out many researches. Though only three continents were known, their territories' positions were unknown for scientists. But in spite of it, there were scientists, who tried to draw lines of the Earth on the map even BC and it proves that geography is one of the ancient sciences.

Travelers, researchers and scientists discover unknown lands and historians write such facts down. Cartographers drew lines of discovered lands in order to present information about discoveries to the society and founded cartography by the way. It isn't difficult to imagine how difficult it was then. Astronomers discovered stars and drew them on the astronomical maps, geographers made maps of discovered lands and travelers went to investigate unknown lands. Travelers and researchers drew discovered unknown lands on the maps they made primitively.

It was very difficult to research regions of Europe and Asia in the Middle Ages. Because, territories, which were interesting for merchants and travelers, were occupied by neighbor countries. The role of ambassadors and merchants was greater than travelers' in investigation of countries, located in the central part of Asia. They brought initial interesting information about unknown countries to the European countries. Every traveler had enough necessary information about Asian countries before travelling to those countries at the end of XV century. Travels of members of Franciscan Order - Giovanni da Pian del Carpine and Benedict of Poland (from Vrotslav) in 1245-1247, member of Dominican Order, monarch Andrew Lanjumon in 1249, member of Franciscan Order Gilliom (Villain) Rubric in 1252-1255, merchants Niccolo and Maffeo Polo from Venice in 1260-1269, Marco Polo in 1271-1295 and Abu Abdullah Muhammad in 1325-1349 towards Eastern Asia, books written about those travels and gathered materials were spread in European countries and were valuable source for people interested in travels.

Art, culture, science and engineering were more developed in the cities, located in the Apennine Peninsula, in comparison with other regions. Even there was serious competition between those cities. There were artists in Florence, ship masters and navigators in Genoa and Venice. Scientists and travelers, who lived in those cities, were interested in geography and astronomy and they learned these fields profoundly. Celebrated traveler Marco Polo from Venice, wellknown astronomer and geographer Paolo Toscanelli from Florentine, travelers Christopher Columbus and Sebastian Cabot from Genoa had been brought up till the end of XV century. The Florentine traveler Giovanni da Verrazzano was able to go down in the history in the first quarter of the 16th century owing to his discoveries.

Though Florence isn't a port city, it could bring up successful astronomer and cosmographer as Amerigo Vespucci.

How could well-known sea travelers as Christopher Columbus, Giovanni Cabot, Sebastian Cabot, Amerigo Vespucci and Giovanni da Verrazzano, be brought up in the cities, located in the Apennine Peninsula during such short time? It should be acknowledged that, these Italians had a significant role in major geographical discoveries and discovery of the New World.

But mentioned sea travelers didn't sail with flags of Venice and Genua. Though they were Italians, worked out of the Apennine Peninsula - Christopher Columbus in Spain, Giovanni Cabot and Sebastian Cabot in England, Amerigo Vespucci in Spain and Portugal, Giovanni da Verrazzano in France.

Strange paradox occurs: Was naval school so weak on the eastern coast of the Atlantic Ocean? Why they couldn't send expeditions under indigenous people's leadership? It isn't a reason. Graduates of Catalonia and Andalusia in Spain, Sagres in Portugal, sea travelers of Brittany and Marseille in France, Bristol and London in England, had great navigation system and they investigated almost all eastern and northern coasts of the Atlantic Ocean.

But mentioned Italian sea travelers could be enough courageous to sail towards territories, located on the other side of the Atlantic Ocean. They were like the Phoenician. It means that, it has another reason. I came to the following conclusion at the result of my researches: They had secret documents and maps proving existence of the forth continent. That's why, they could gain major successes in the history of geographical discoveries.

The rich materials gathered at the result of the geographical discoveries, ended lasting stagnation in the field of geography and explained obscurities and wrong ideas.[1]

Activities of mentioned sea travelers had a great role in introduction of North and South America to the Old World. Which factor influenced improvement of those people?

There were well-known sea travelers in Portugal, who could overcome transatlantic expeditions.

The difference between Pyreness and Apennine Peninsulas: Italian sea travelers regularly traveled to the countries, located in the east of the Mediterranean Sea, including Iran, Central Asia and Chine, but Portuguese sea travelers investigated western coasts of Africa. The Spanish, who were busy with Reconquista (freeing Spain from Arabians), travelled only to Canaries.

The Genoese and Venetians, who competed with each others for hegemony on the Mediterranean Sea, gave

[1] T. Həsənov, Ə. Hacızadə. Coğrafiya tarixi, Bakı Univesitetinin Nəşriyyatı. Milli Virtual Kitabxana. Bakı, 2001 səh. 25.

special importance to cartography, got different maps from Arabian and Turkish seamen and worked a lot to improve them.

Science and education centers had been founded in Florence, Bologna, Padua and Pizza and their leading scientists began to investigate scientific works of Muslim scientists in the Near East. As the astronomy, mathematics, geography and cartography were developed speedily in the East, these scientists' works were interesting for scientists of the West. Scientists of the East learned about existence of the forth continent first, gave initial information about it and could attract attention of the scientists of the West.

The West was interested in India, which was full of gold, jewel and spices and neighboring regions. Land routes to this country, which was considered world of tales, were under control of Turks and Muslims. So, Christians, who didn't want to pay taxes to Muslims, had to think about alternative routes. That's why, they discovered the forth continent, which was unknown for a long time, in 1492 as tried to discover lands around the Atlantic Ocean.

Discovery of the western route to India consists of five stages. The first stage covers 1415-1434, second

1434-1362, third 1470-1475 and the forth covers 1482-1487. The fifth stage began in 1497.

Paolo dal Pozzo Toscanelli (1397-1484) was well-known enough in the second half of the 15th century and his fame had got over the borders of the Apennine Peninsula. It isn't strange that, captains and navigators asked him for advice when were going to travel. Christopher Columbus also worked with Paolo Toscanelli, before he became conqueror of seas and ocean. Same things may be said about Amerigo Vespucci too. Perhaps, he was interested in astronomy and geography owing to the Florentine scientist. Both of them were known as cosmographers in the world.

Vespucci, who was enough professional in his job, had promised to realize the most sensational discovery in order to be remembered together with Marco Polo and Cadamosto. It is known that, the Florentine accountant could keep his promise.

How is it possible? How can a man, who hadn't any significant role in major geographical discoveries, be remembered together with the most celebrated sea travelers? How could Amerigo Vespucci gain this fame? He had to have enough information in order to make the world to believe him. Why did leading scientists didn't analyze his claims? Who was responsible for this confusion? Amerigo Vespucci or scientists, who allowed his lie to be spread?

Scientists of Europe only watched events happening around. But the lie continued broaden its activity. It could be possible by making some planned steps. Scientists weren't so credulous then. Some background was needed for it. He had to make the world to believe that, the New World was discovered by Amerigo Vespucci, not by Columbus. He became more popular than Christopher Columbus, Bartolomeu Dias, Vasco da Gama, Vicente Yáñez Pinzón, Alonso de Ojeda, Juan de la Cosa, Pedro Alonso (Peralonso) Nino and other sea travelers, who had a significant role in major geographical discoveries. He achieved it owing his madeup letters, published by different publishers. Researches proved that, letters spread in Europe by Vespucci, didn't contain his real memories, they were copies of information given by other travelers. He simply gathered and spread mentioned information.

There isn't any confusion and investigations proved that, the letters spread in Europe under Vespucci's name, didn't include facts seen by him during the travels, but they were forged letters prepared using materials of other travelers. He simply gathered all facts and presented to the society by means of some emissaries.

I had to look through events, happened 520 years ago, and describe corresponding processes in order to find out the truth. So, justice could win at last.

Christopher Columbus's travel to Spain

As Columbus lost his hopes in Portugal, he decided to go to Castilia in 1485. He took his seven-years-old on Diego to Palos and wanted to leave him in Huelva, near relatives of his wife. Besides it, he sent his brother Bartolommeo to England and asked him to take plan of the western way to India to Heinrich VII. Columbus hoped that, the king of England will be interested in the plan.

As Columbus was very tired, he entered Rabid monastery in order to rest. He talked to the owner of the monastery Antonio de Marchena (he was interested in geography and cosmography) about his secret. Antonio got excited when heard Columbus's thoughts. As he had relations with the kingdom palace, he sent traveler to authoritative persons and introduced him to the Herzog Medina Sidonia. Herzog promised Columbus to support his plan, but didn't keep his promise.

Columbus was very happy as was met sincerely in the monastery. He went to Cordova afterwards. Then Ferdinand from Aragon and Isabella from Castilia lived in Cordova.

But Cristobal Colon (Christopher Columbus was called Cristobal Colon in Spain) was disappointed in Spain. Consultants of the king declared his plan unreal.

Of course, there wasn't any need to explain the reason. Monarchs were busy with the war against Granada - the small country of Arabs located in Spain. Columbus knew that rulers of Spain wouldn't be interested in his plan until Arabs would be defeated. So, he took his project to England and Portugal. But both of these countries rejected his project.

Antonio de Marchena introduced Columbus to Herzog von Medinaceli, who was respected by Spanish monarchs and had several vessels in the port Puerto-Santa-Maria and don Luis de la Cerda. Herzog was interested in the project. He promised to help the traveler. But such presentations were harmful for Columbus's plan. Herzog asked Isabella to allow organization of corresponding expedition. The queen hesitated. The expedition's success may help large feudalists - her enemies to be stronger. She had to spend a lot of money for organization of the expedition. And there wasn't any guarantee for success of the expedition. If it would fail, the queen would lose a lot of money, but if it would succeed, the kingdom would become richer and stronger. So, the queen invited Columbus to her palace in Cordova on May 1, 1486 and after a short discussion, presented his project to the commission.

The queen Isabella was clever, haughty and decisive ruler. She liked Columbus's presentation and promised that, would help him. Columbus was sure that, he would travel to the west of the ocean soon.

The commission consisting of monarchs and noblemen made negative decision after four years under the leadership of Isabella's godfather Fernando Talavera. The commission gathered twice in Cordova and Salamanca. One of meetings was leaded by Diego de Deza, who was future archbishop of Seville and owner of the Dominican Order. Diego de Deza tried to prove that, Columbus's calculations were wrong.

Original copy of the commission's decision hasn't remained until today. But it is known that, members of the commission explained their decisions by means of different reasons. They didn't mention that, the Earth wasn't spherical. Though their decision was negative, they couldn't explain their thoughts completely. Though the commission's decision was negative, Columbus got salary of the kingdom in 1487-1488. But he couldn't achieve any success during this time.

Christopher Columbus went to the kingdom camp located in Malaga with the invitation of Spanish monarchs in August and September of 1487. Malaga had been occupied on August 18, 1487 after a long blockade. Columbus thought that, Isabella will agree to organize an expedition. But the queen mentioned that, any expedition couldn't be organized until the Iberian Peninsula would be freed of Arabs.

So, Columbus readdressed to Portugal in 1488, but was rejected. As you know, Bartolommeo Columbus was sent to London, to Heinrich VII by his brother. He asked the king to support Columbus's ideas and organize an expedition. But the king's consultants didn't accept his idea. They appealed to France too, but couldn't succeed.

Then Bartolommeo stayed in Fontainebleau and worked as a cartographer.

Herzog Medinaceli wanted to organize Columbus's expedition, but rulers' permission was necessary for it. Herzog respected the Genoese sea traveler and Columbus stayed in Medinaceli's house until the commission's decision was made. But sometimes he visited Cordova and there he got acquainted with the young girl by name Beatriz de Arana, who was for 15 years younger than he. Their son Ferdinand (future biographer of the traveler) was born there. Ferdinand was traveler's illegitimate child, as Columbus and his mother weren't married. Their marriage could prevent Columbus's success. But he respected his family.

According to historical sources, Columbus had ordered his son Diego to send 10000 maravedis rente to Beatriz annually since 1502. Diego had to support welfare of Beatriz after 1506 too. The traveler was very kind to Beatriz and her family. Her brother Pedro de Arana leaded one of caravels of the expedition during the traveler's third travel and cousin participated in the first travel.

The vice-king of America Diego always sent Beatrice's annual rente and fixed it in his will. After his death, his wife continued sending that rente (Diego's wife was the daughter of the Spanish nobleman) to the family of Arana.

Columbus was a sagacious person and understood that, Spanish rulers wouldn't help him until they would achieve their goals. He waited for the end of the war between Arabs and Spain. He began to be close to Spanish financers and it helped him on his way to the victory. Christopher Columbus returned to Rabid monastery in 1491 and got acquainted with the well-known shipbuilder Martin Alonso Pinson with the help of Antonio de Marchena. Besides it, he developed relations with the king's financial counselor, merchants and bankers of Seville.

Some skeptics and scientists mention that, Columbus discovered America by accident. So, that discovery could be made by any captain. Of course, I don't agree with this assumption.

Columbus didn't lose his courage and read a lot of scientific books in order to prepare for the expedition. He mainly read books on geography and cosmography. Especially, he read Marco Polo's books and made a lot of notes about them. He was sure that, his considerations were correct. Besides it, he had Pliny's **"Natural** history" in an Italian translation published in 1489, works of Plutarch and Ptolemy. He made notes on several books as Pierre de Ailly's **"Imaqo Mundi" ("World Map")** and Enea Silvia Piccolomini's (is known as the Pope Pius II) **"Historia rerum ubique Mundi"** besides Marco Polo's book written in Latin, which is still kept in the Columbia Library of Seville. There are about 2125 notes made by him.[1]

Pierre de Ailly wrote a tractate on general geography in 1410. He supported ideas of Marinus of Tyre, who thought that, Asia extended towards the east and there was only a narrow ocean between Asia and Europe. The French cosmographer even wrote that, it was possible to pass that ocean in several days when the weather was fine. The Genoese seaman underlined this sentence and made detailed note about it. He made notes about the sentence, where the author of **"Imaqo Mundi"** wrote that, Spain isn't very far from India and the east starts near the west. Chapters about India and Asia are full of notes. It seems that, pictures of valuable stones and metals, elephants and different terrible animals amazed

---

[1] Ч. Верлинден. Покорители Америки. Ростов-на-Дону, «Феникс», 1997. стр. 32.

Columbus. He fixed places, which were full of pearls. Besides it, he described narrow places of the ocean with different color in his map.

He underlined one of paragraphs in Enea Silvia Piccolomini's **"Historia rerum",** where the author wrote that, Asia extended towards the latitude of Spain. He noted on other paragraph, where the author described Chinese as peaceful creatures, that, Chine is situated near India, on the other side of Spain and Ireland.

J. Baker wrote that, Columbus's cosmographical ideas were founded in the middle ages. He used the book of Pierre de Ailli - *"Tractatus de imagine mundi" (Tractate about the description of the Earth*), which included thoughts of Roger Bacon described in *"Opus Magus"* at the end of XIII century. So, Columbus hadn't any new ideas.[1]

Columbus was interested in the Mongol emperor of Chine, who was the leader in 18 places, but Enea Silvio described Khubilay khan in his work. All these facts prove that, the traveler was interested in the western way to Asia.

---

[1] Дж. Бейкер. История географических открытий и исследований. Пер. с англ.М., «Иностранной литература», 1950. IV глава.

Thus, it is obvious that, Columbus spent his free time in reading scientific books and tried to learn different science branches. Even captains and navigators couldn't overcome the work carried out by Columbus. He was a passionate researcher, could plan the future, learn navigation, use Passats, learn climate changes in the east of the Atlantic Ocean, use the Sun, Moon and Venus for determination of geographic coordinates, treat people kindly and lead dialogues. Probably, coasts of the New World could be discovered in 100-150 years. It's a reality. Several seamen tried to cross the ocean in the west before Columbus. But their expeditions failed. These facts can be proved.

Calculations of the Florentine cosmographer Paolo Toscanelli brought about a fundamental change in Columbus's life

There were experienced captains, cosmographers, navigators, boatswain and seamen in Portugal and seamen became skilful experts in expeditions. But there was a great need for professional seamen in Spain and so, most navigation leaders didn't want to lose skilful travelers as Christopher Columbus. And the traveler mentioned that, Spain would use his skill and experience one day.

Columbus corresponded with the Florentine scientist Paolo Toscanelli before traveling to coasts of Guinea. Two letters sent by the scientist to the Genoese seaman were very important for him.

According to most historical sources, Ch. Columbus asked Paolo Toscanelli's advice in 1474. This advice was about the short seaway to India. The Florentine scientist was known as a great expert of cosmography in Italy and Portugal then. He corresponded with most colleagues, who lived in other cities, about his works.

Every innovation made in the middle ages was investigated by progressive minded people. Especially, geographical discoveries were very interesting for people. After the Venetian merchant Marco Polo traveled to Chine, sea travelers of Portugal began to investigate unknown places located in the east of the Atlantic Ocean and some changes of the Earth began to be discovered. Most cartographers began to describe new territories on their maps and presented it to the world community. It was very profitable business. Such experts had relations with sea travelers and geographers. Changes of the Earth's structure were interesting for churchmen too. The canonic of a temple located in Lisbon by name Fernan Martins was a plenipotentiary agent of the king of Portugal Alfonso V in Rome and there he had got acquainted with Paolo Toscanelli. He asked questions about the Earth's measurements and distance between the western coast of Europe and eastern coast of Asia.

Paolo Toscanelli used measurements of Marco Polo rather than measurements of the well-known Greek scientist Claudio Ptolemy when he prepared the project about the Earth's measurement. But other scientists – most geographers and cosmographers used measurements of the well-known Greek scientist. Marco Polo had described coasts of Asia at 30^0 towards the east unlike the Greek scientist.

Measurements determined by Toscanelli were interesting for the king of Portugal Alfonso V too. Fernan Martins corresponded with the Florentine scientist after he returned to Lisbon in accordance with the king's order. Christopher Columbus also corresponded with his fellow countryman. The Florentine cosmographer had sent the copy of the letter written to F.

Martins to Columbus either. He wrote that, there was a shorter way by passing the Atlantic Ocean in the west besides the way to Spice Islands (Moluccas). *"I know that it is possible to prove existence of this way if the Earth will be considered spherical. I send my map in order to simplify your work. Route of sailing to the west, necessary islands and coasts and point of destination have been described on that map. Distances from equator and pole have also been written. I have described countries of spices and valuable stones in the west though they are usually described in the east. Those places can be reached in the east by going on the land..."*

Christopher Columbus was interested in navigation since his early years. He thought a lot before working on important issues. He always desired to participate in great expeditions. Probably Columbus informed Paolo Toscanelli about his project. He wrote to the Genoese sea traveler: *"I congratulate you for your decision to sail to the east from the west. I am glad that, you have understood me".*

I think that, Christopher Columbus couldn't agree with thoughts of the Florentine cosmographer. First of all, well-known sea traveler couldn't agree with length of the Earth's outline. It means that, Asia isn't situated in the Atlantic Ocean at 10000-12000 km away from Canaries in the west as Paolo Toscanelli thought. Columbus had determined that, land area located in the west of the Atlantic Ocean was at 4500-5000 km away from Europe. It means that, the mentioned land was other land, which was unknown for the Old World.

Toscanelli was a defender and leader of the public library founded by the humanist Niccolo Niccolini. He defended ideas mentioning that, the Earth is spherical and planned to go to India through the western way. The astronomer had edited *"Table of Alfonso"* (XIII century). Though Toscanelli had read scientific works of most scientists, he had lessened measurements of the Earth for unknown results.

Experts can't justify Toscanelli for such rude mistake. He had made elementary mistakes when made his map in 1474. But he had opportunities for preventing those mistakes. The Greek scientist Eratosthenes lived in Alexandria. According to his calculations, the length of the Earth's outline was 43625 km and its radius was 6943 km.[1] There is no doubt that, Columbus knew this

---

[1] R. Qasımov. Konkistadorların Mərkəzi Çili sahillərində faciəli ölümü.

fact. As he was interested in astronomy, he had taken into account calculations of Eratosthenes, Poseidon, Al-Khwarizmi, Al-Biruni, Tusi and Toscanelli before starting his travel.

Usually cupolas of temples were used as part of sun watches. The most popular example is the cupola of Santa Maria del Fiore located in Florentine. Paolo Toscanelli installed his popular gnomon in the temple in 1474 and could determine afternoon moment by means of it with exactness of half a second.

He attached a bronze plate with a hole in the middle of it on the window located on 90 m and made a ruler on the floor in the left of the main church. Rays of the Sun passed through the hole of the disk and reached the floor in two months - between the end of May and end of June. The device had remained until the end of XIX century and then was destroyed by restorers by mistake.

At the result of inexactness of measurements, Toscanelli lessened measurements of the Earth and determined that, the distance between Spain and India was 6 thousand miles - this measurement was two times less than the real measurement.

Bakı, "Çaşıoğlu", 1999. səh. 247.

The French physician Jan Fernell (1497-1558), who was interested in astronomy, wrote that, the length of the Earth's outline was 39816 km and its radius was 6337 km.[1] It means that, Toscanelli had made a mistake. According to his calculations, the length of the Earth's outline was 29000 km. So, Columbus didn't accept report of the Florentine scientist and took into account measurements determined by the Greek scientist Eratosthenes and geographic coordinates determined by Nasiraddin Tusi.

Of course, my hypothesis is serious enough. As N. Tusi's map was kept in the library of Florentine, *"Zij-i Ilkhani"* also might be kept there. How could Columbus find that work then?

It means that, Columbus got acquainted with Paolo Toscanelli when he was in Portugal. But he knew the Florentine scientist when he was in Italy. They say that, Columbus met Toscanelli in Italy and discussed interesting issues with him... The Genoese traveler was interested in the scientist's works and liked to look through his maps.

---

[1] О. Коротцев. Глобус, как измеряли землю. Ленинград, «Д.Л», 1980. стр. 312.

Toscanelli liked to share his ideas with his friends unlike other scientists. But he kept his sources secret as didn't want other scientists to steel his discoveries. I want to look through a brief historical chronology before analyzing this issue. It concerns Paolo Toscanelli's activity.

Nobody knew how lands and oceans joined each-others in the Earth. Though Toscanelli was a scientist, he described Asia for two times larger and ocean between South Europe and Chine narrower. According to his calculations, the distance between Europe and Chine was 2000 liq (12000 km). Cipango (Japan) was situated at about 333 liq (1998-2000) in the east of Chine. Azores, Canaries and Anthelia could be used as stopping places during the passage. Columbus made his calculations in accordance with books of astronomy and geography. He thought that, it was necessary to travel for 800 liq (4.5-5 thousand km) in the west from Canaries to East Asia in order to go to Cipango. This was a phenomenal idea. The French geographer of XVIII century Jan Anvil wrote about it: *"This was a mistake and it resulted in great discovery"*.

Did Columbus make the greatest discovery of the world owing to this mistake? Isn't it a miracle? It may mean that: America was discovered in 1492 by the expedition of Columbus by accident. But this assumption can't be accepted. The discovery of the global importance can't be made by accident.

According to books of history and geography, Christopher Columbus thought until the end of his life that, he had discovered East Asia. It was mentioned in our textbooks too. Only pessimist people can believe it. Most people don't believe this assumption. But they don't investigate facts and only mention that it is an arguable problem. I also can't accept this assumption and so, began to investigate corresponding events. Of course, it is difficult to believe that, the experienced admiral and professional traveler as Christopher Columbus didn't understand that, he had discover coasts of the New World though he had traveled there for four times. But most experts write that it is a truth.

Columbus got acquainted with the map made by the Florentine scientist Toscanelli in 1474 when he was in Italy. I want to mention that, the distance between Canaries and Bahamas is about 950 liq. According to Columbus's calculations, the most convenient way to Cipango (Japan) was 800 liq towards East Asia in the west of Canaries. It seems that, Columbus didn't take

Toscanelli's map into consideration after he made his own calculations. He didn't need the Florentine scientist's calculations.

There was another unknown map besides Paolo Toscanelli's map. I think, the Genoese admiral made his own map by means of most scientists' calculations and that unknown map and used it during his travel. He had enough information when reached coasts of the New World by means of the Canary current and Passats, so, he couldn't think that, those lands were Asia. As it was mentioned above, he had prepared seriously for the expedition towards Spain and hadn't shared his ideas with anybody besides his brother. He knew that, there weren't unknown eastern coasts of Asia on the other side of the Atlantic Ocean.

Discovery of America and secrets brought to light during that travel

I want to mention some facts in order to analyze that discovery. There are different assumptions about the purpose of Columbus's expedition. Some literatures even say that, Columbus didn't aim to reach coasts of Asia in 1492. The agreement signed by Christopher Columbus and two monarchs should be analyzed in order to understand it. He could get all privileges and titles, which he wanted, only in accordance with the order of Spanish monarchs after the discovery would be made. There wasn't name of any place in the agreement. But it had other reason.

After the Pope divided the Earth between Castilia and Portugal in 1479, Portuguese seamen could travel towards south and east of Canaries and seamen of Castilia could travel towards the west and north. So, monarchs of Castilia couldn't speak about any part of Asia. That territory was under Portuguese's control. It should be mentioned that, mentioned agreement could be about Asia only. Then, people all over the world thought that there was Asia on the other side of the Atlantic Ocean. That is, Asia was situated in east and west of Europe. That's why Columbus sailed towards the west as soon as he left the Hierro Island. Besides it, the expedition had to bring pearls, valuable stones, gold, silver and spices from discovered land in accordance with concluded agreement. India was considered motherland of such goods then.

İ. P. Magidovich and V. I. Magidovich write in II volume of **"Historical essays on geographical discoveries":** "The expedition wasn't organized for occupation of territories, it was organized for creation of commercial relations with discovered countries. Columbus's expedition had to establish commercial relations with discovered non-Christian countries (Muslim) and try to appropriate discovered islands. There weren't professional fighters and enough weapons in the expedition and it proved that, the expedition wouldn't realize serious military operations. Besides it, the expedition didn't plan to spread Christianity in discovered lands, though Columbus had tried to achieve it. There wasn't any churchman and monarch in the expedition, there was only the Jewish converted to Christianity, who knew Arabian".[1]

---

[1] И. П. Магидович, В. И. Магидович. Очерки по истории географических открытий, II том. Москва, "Просвещение", 1982. стр. 25.

It should be mentioned that, Arabian wasn't needed in Brazil or Anthelia Islands. It could be needed in East Asia as it was Muslims' common language. It means that, the expedition planned to reach India and its neighbours in accordance with the agreement concluded between Christopher Columbus and monarchs. Monarchs' main purpose was to establish commercial relations with India.

According to official chronics, after the first travel (1493), Columbus declared that, he had discovered India in the west of Europe and brought several Hindus from there. Columbus believed that he had reached the place where he wanted to go. Organizers of the first expedition also thought so. That's why they began to organize a great expedition. There weren't skeptics then, and they appeared afterwards.

Portuguese didn't believe that, Columbus could reach East Asia. Some scientists analyzed the route of Columbus's expedition and didn't believe that the Earth's outline was so short. There were skeptics in Spain then. The Italian humanist Pietro Martire (Poignant Peter), who lived in Barcelona and were close to the kingdom palace, corresponded with his fellow-countrymen. He had written in the letter written on

November 1, 1493: *"One person by name Colon (Columbus) says that, he could reach India, the place of antipodes of the west. He discovered many islands located on the other side of the East Ocean near India as cosmographers thought... I don't want to write anything about it, nevertheless size of the Earth made me to think otherwise"*.

That is, before the travel of Christopher Columbus, Pietro Martire thought otherwise about calculations of Paolo Toscanelli. So, Columbus also might think as Pietro Martire, but not as Paolo Toscanelli.

I think that, Christopher Columbus couldn't agree with thoughts of the Florentine cosmographer. First of all, well-known sea traveler couldn't agree with length of the Earth's outline. It means that, Asia isn't situated in the Atlantic Ocean at 10000-12000 km away from Canaries in the west as Paolo Toscanelli thought. Columbus had determined that, land area located in the west of the Atlantic Ocean was at 4500-5000 km away from Europe. It means that, the mentioned land was other land, which was unknown for the Old World. I think, he agreed with ideas of the Azerbaijani scientist after getting acquainted with Nasiraddin Tusi's **"Zij-i Ilkhani"** and his map and was sure that, the land area located in the west of the Atlantic Ocean was at 4500-5000 km away from Europe. That distance could be overcome in 30-35 days.

The Italian scientist and humanist, cosmographer and astronomer Toscanelli (1397 – Florentine – May 10, 1482) was the defender and leader of the public library founded by the humanist Niccolo Niccolini. He defended ideas mentioning that, the Earth is spherical and planned to go to India through the western way. The astronomer had edited **"Table of Alfonso"** (XIII century). Though Toscanelli had read scientific works of most scientists, he had lessened measurements of the Earth for unknown results. The Florentine scientist could make a mistake. It was difficult to find the length of the Earth's outline then. The French physician Jan Ferrell (1497-1558), who was interested in astronomy, could determine exact length of the Earth's outline. It means that, Toscanelli had made a mistake.

I can't justify Toscanelli for such rude mistake. He had made elementary mistakes when made his map in 1474. But he had opportunities for preventing those mistakes. The Greek scientist Eratosthenes lived in Alexandria founded by Macedonian Isgandar in 332 BC.

That city attracted scientists and travelers of the world then.

According to his calculations, the length of the Earth's outline was 43625 km and its radius was 6943 km. There is no doubt that, Columbus knew this fact. As he was interested in astronomy, he had taken into account calculations of Eratosthenes, Poseidon, Al-Khwarizmi, Al-Biruni, Tusi and Toscanelli before starting his travel. He planned to achieve success and to go down in history unlike other travelers who tried to find land in the west of the Atlantic Ocean.

The French physician Jan Ferrell wrote that, the length of the Earth's outline was 39816 km and its radius was 6337 km.[1] It means that, Toscanelli had made a mistake. According to his calculations, the length of the Earth's outline was 29000 km. I think that, Columbus had read at least part of **"Zij-i Ilkhani"** written by Nasiraddin Tusi before his travel. Then, important scientific works, especially works on astronomy and the Earth's measurements were translated and sold to scientists with very high prices. Columbus, who was

---

[1] О. Коротцев. Глобус, как измеряли землю. Ленинград, «Д.Л», 1980. стр. 312.

preparing for the important expedition, had got acquainted with Nasiraddin Tusi's map besides **"Zij-i Ilkhani"** and protected that map with all his forces. Measurements and outlines described in mentioned map could influence on the result of the expedition. That's why the traveler didn't agree with the Florentine scientist's report and used measurements and outlines determined by Eratosthenes and Tusi.

Of course, my hypothesis is serious enough. Nasiraddin Tusi's map was kept in the library of Florentine and Paolo Toscanelli leaded that library. I think, Toscanelli couldn't give that material to Columbus. Though they knew each-others, the scientist didn't show that material to anybody. But it is obvious that, Columbus had used that map when passed the ocean. How could Columbus find that map then?

Vespucci realizes his scenario

As it was mentioned above, the first letter was written to one of the influential persons of Florentine – Lorenzo di Pierfrancesco de' Medici at the end of 1502 or in March-April of 1503. He prepared the letter hastily in order to be one of the well-known travelers. Because, that mission hadn't achieved any serious success.

The fact that, the land discovered by Columbus was the fourth continent of the Earth, which wasn't known in the Old World, gradually began to be spread. This was officially declared by Juan de la Cosa – participant of the first expedition of Christopher Columbus. It was a sensetional discovery. Vespucci had to misappropriate the Genoese admiral's success.

Vespucci was lucky. When Columbus discovered outfall of the Orinoco during his third travel (1498-1500), he understood that, such rich river could belong to the continent only. If that territory wasn't part of Asia, it could be unknown continent. But that success wasn't good for monarchs and officials of Spain. They hadn't planned such great discovery. So, intrigues against the Genoese admiral began to be prepared after that news spread in Spain.

At first, he had to be disgraced. The most suitable condition for it was rebellion of the Spanish Hidalgos and other missioners against the brothers of Columbus in Hispaniola (Haiti). The Spanish monarchs tried to use this suitable condition. Their representative Francisco de Bobadilla was sent to Hispaniola with special competencies and he led interrogation without questioning brothers of Columbus. Besides, Nicolás de Ovando was appointed governor of the island. Columbus and his brothers were arrested and sent to Spain in handcuffs at the beginning of 1500.

In 1499, after preconceived explanations of Francisco de Bobadilla sent to Spain, monopoly of Columbus on the New World was lost and new expeditions began to be sent towards the Caribbean Sea. Vespucci used this opportunity and prepared his second letter. He wrote that, he had participated at four travels in 1497-1504. He didn't need any witness to prove it. Because that forged letter had to be published far from the Pyreness Peninsula.

Why did Vespucci do it? He tried to misappropriate several successes with one letter. Columbus reached the southern continent of the New World in 1498. Vespucci wrote that, he reached mentioned coast first of all in 1497 and besides, investigated that territory. In addition, he wrote that as if he investigated a large territory (between Honduras and southeastern coasts of Mexico), which was considered bridge between two continents, located in the west of the Central America. It means that, he wanted to show that discovery as his success. Though according to the historical sources, that territory was discovered by Columbus in 1503-1504 and large report was sent to the Spanish monarchs about it.

If Vespucci was right, we could say that, mentioned lands were discovered by him. But the Florentine accountant unmasked himself as he didn't consider actual processes, prohibitions on travelers and their political positions. How could Vespucci or other Spanish traveler sail to the western part of the Atlantic Ocean in 1497 when monopoly on the coasts of the New World belonged to Columbus before 1499? It means that, Vespucci lied. The second lie of the second letter was on the investigation of coasts of Honduras and Mexico. He only tried to misappropriate successes of Columbus. Could Vespucci do it on somebody's request?

Of course, the rebellion of the Spanish Hidalgos against brothers of Columbus organized in 1498 wasn't good for the admiral and his opponents tried to use this opportunity effectively. But there was an agreement between Christopher Columbus and Spanish monarchs and everybody had to consider it. That's why Columbus had to be disgraced and deprived of his fame. Vespucci appeared in that stage.

The governor of Hispaniola ordered Nicolas de Ovando not to allow the admiral to enter the island in 1502, when Columbus started his fourth travel. It means that, Columbus was persona non grata for the Spanish authority. Though the capital of the island Santo Domingo was founded by the admiral in 1494 (Santo Domingo was considered the first city of the New World by Europeans). Even nobody helped Columbus when he met an accident in Jamaica and Ovando said that he had to die in front of the sea. Of course, the governor sent information on the miserable fate of the Genoese traveler, who was discoverer of the New World, to his supporters in Madrid. Vespucci's forged letters began to spread during that period. His purpose was to declare himself discoverer of the New World.

I explained it above in detail.

Vespucci mentioned that, he was invited to the expedition by the king Ferdinand during the first travel. He didn't write anything about his position during the second travel and wrote that he was an assistant of captains during other two travels. But nobody confirmed these appointments. He wrote almost nothing about geographical coordinates (especially latitudes) and navigation calculations. But Vespucci described starry sky of the southern hemisphere, nature of discovered countries, outward appearances, characters, culture and traditions of Hindus with special enthusiasm. Of course, he had stolen all this information.

There was great interest for discovered countries and lands in Europe in those years. Reports of the travelers and navigators were rarely published. That's why Vespucci's letters on his "travels" caused great interest in most countries of Europe.

Some experts came to the conclusion that, most sentences were added to the letters by other people, especially publishers and Vespucci didn't know anything about it. The purpose was to cause interest. That's why, Vespucci's letters were translated into different languages and published for twenty-thre times during a short time.

There is a fact of such interference. Holland publisher published report of Vespucci's fifth travel a year later – in 1508. He used notes of Balthasar Sprenger for preparation of that forged report and that manuscript was spread widely. The publisher only replaced the phrase "Ego, Balthasar Sprenger" (I, Balthasar Sprenger in

Latin) of the original manuscript with the phrase "İck, Alberigus" (I, Alberigus in Latin) in order to make readers believe that, it was really Vespucci's travel. Such forgery could mislead even the chairman of the London Geographic Society 400 years later. In 1892, he grandiloquently declared that, Vespucci's fifth travel was found out.[1]

Defenders of the Florentine accountant mentioned that, he wasn't aware of such frauds. But I have some doubts on this issue. It doesn't convincing that Vespucci knew nothing about such tumultuous publicization. Because he was head navigator of Castile and there were a lot of secret employees of his organization in big cities of Europe. How could they forget to inform the head navigator? Were they busy with doing Amerigo Vespucci's other bidding in Europe? May be, they tried to spread forged documents on the discovery of the fourth continent?

Many objective specialists wrote about Vespucci's inactivity. S. Sveyg wrote: "Why didn't Vespucci deny books published under his name though he died in 1512?

---

[1] С. Цвейг. Собрание сочинений в семи томах. Звездные часы человечества. III том. Москва, «Правда», 1963. стр. 438-439.

Could he knew nothing about that fake propaganda? Wasn't he able to declare that wasn't discoverer of America?" [1]

All these facts prove that, Vespucci deceived the world community owing to mentioned letters.

Why didn't most scientists unmask Vespucci's lie? Perhaps, nobody couldn't dare to do it or didn't pay attention to this problem. Because Vespucci was appointted head navigator of Castile two years after death of the Genoese traveler and made most scientists, especially geographers of Spain to depend on him using his authority. So, those persons began to gather materials for the head navigator.

After a while, those persons began to declare that Vespucci was discoverer of the coasts of the New World. Only a group of people knew that it was a lie. But most of them had a significant role in making it to look like truth. If they tried to unmask Vespucci, they would also be unmasked. Nobody could dare to do it. It could end their carrier completely. So those persons were obliged to support Vespucci even after his death. Vespucci had

[1] С. Цвейг. Собрание сочинений в семи томах. Звездные часы человечества. III том. Москва, «Правда», 1963. стр. 439.

planned it beforehand. But in spite of it, Waldsemuller named discovered land *"Unknown land"* instead of *"America"* when he published map of the coasts of the New World in 1517. Though that map was considered copy of the map, which was made in 1507 and was demonstrated in Sen-Dye. Did the scientist become more honest or had it another reason?

There is no doubt that, Waldsemuller tried to restore the truth. Because naming Vespucci well-known traveler though he hadn't role in discovery of the New World was deceiving the world community. There were pressures on the family of Columbus in order to steal the fame of the well-known Genoese traveler.

Intrigues against Christopher Columbus

Scientists wanted to note that Columbus wasn't the first traveler, who reached coasts of the New World. They mentioned that, some Europeans sailed there before him and the Genoese seaman knew it already. It was said in order to hide success achieved by Columbus. Because his discovery didn't please leaders of Spain.

Columbus was very ambitious person and required great privileges of the Spanish monarchs before starting his first transatlantic travel and that's why aroused hatred in many persons. Why didn't he suppose that those privileges could harm him? This step can be characterized as a prescience or risk. Perhaps, he wanted to be only leader of discovered lands. But Columbus earned a lot of enemies owing to this step.

After discovery of the fourth continent for Spain and whole Old World, Columbus required his privileges and he was sure that would be able to get them. Of course, the Spanish monarchs Isabella of Castile and Ferdinand of Aragon had to keep their promises. But as the privileges were so great, this step could make Columbus third or fourth person of the kingdom. It wasn't convincing that, the Spanish officials would allow progress of the Italian traveler. So, Christopher Columbus had to be disgraced and there were too many methods for it.

Those actions were started after the admiral's third travel and culmination occurred after he died. Of course, heirs of the admiral struggled against the Spanish monarchs in order to defend their legal rights.

I want to note several moments of the campaign against the admiral.

Half of Florida, Anthill islands, Mexico and South America became property of Portugal after the treaty of Alcáçovas was signed between Portugal and Spain in 1481. After **"Aeterni Regis"** came into force, historians began to write that, America was discovered by the Portugal travelers before 1481 and they kept this fact secret for a long time. This idea was supported by all chroniclers of the 16th century – Bartolomé de las Casas, Francisco López de Gómara and Gonzalo Fernández de Oviedo y Valdés. The Peruvian chronicler Garcilaso de la Vega (son of the Hidalgo from Extremadura and Ink prince) even noted that, discoverer of America was Alonso Sánchez de Huelva. Besides, George Blon, Francisco López de Gómara Alonso and others wrote that, Huelva had met with Columbus.

I have to list following facts in order to prove it:

Alonso Sánchez de Huelva, who was from Niebla, carried different goods from Spain to Canaries in 1484 with his small vessel. He took fruits from Canaries to Madeira and went to Spain with jams. He was met by hurricane on his way between Canaries and Madeira. He sailed for 28 or 29 days under the hurricane and approached unknown island by accident. Perhaps, it was Santo Domingo as it is located on the route of the hurricane (east wind).[1]

Ones a wrecked vessel approached the coast of Porto Santo. Columbus noticed one weakened navigator among survived seamen. One of seamen raved about songs of motley birds, unknown animals and colored people. The vessel had been sailing from the west and struck the coast. Christopher Columbus took half-dead navigator home. He looked after his guest and it became clear that, navigator's name was Alonso Sanchez de Huelva. After getting better, Alonso Sanchez explained everything that happened to them. It became clear that, they had lost their way in the dark sea (then Atlantic Ocean was called like that – R. D.) and reached very charming island. Sanchez informed his liberator about the place where the island was situated.[1] After it he died as other survived seamen of the wrecked vessel.[2]

---

[1] Горсиласо де ла Вега. Текст воспроизведен по изданию, История государства Инков. Л. «Наука». 1974. стр. 16-17.

[1] Жорж Блон, «Атлантический океан», стр. 15.

[2] Франциско-де-Гомара. «Общая история Индий», 1552 г., XIII

According to the Peruvian chronicler Garcilaso de la Vega, historian Francisco Lopez de Gomara had written about the adventure of Alonso Sanchez de Huelva in his work "General history of India". Son of the Ink prince caviled at that work as following: "De Gomara heard this information from ordinary persons - seamen and civil people, his father and father's authoritative friends, including people, who were close to the palace".

This adventure was told by the bishop Joseph Acosta for the first time. When he was in Peru, he heard that, one seaman had discovered coasts of the New World at the result of heavy hurricane and showed the way to Christopher Columbus as the Genoese seaman helped him after the catastrophe happened on the way to Madeira. Columbus told this story to some acquaintances including courtiers, and they helped him in organization of the expedition.[1]

Conquistadors noted that, America had been discovered by Alonso Sanchez (de Huelva – R. D.). It was said because there was an inheritance conflict between heirs of Columbus and leadership of Castilia at that time

глава, «Первая открытия Индии».

[1] Горсиласо де ла Вега. Текст воспроизведен по изданию, История государства Инков. Л. «Наука». 1974. стр. 17-18.

(1510-1550). That's why courtiers tried to prove that, lands located on the other side of the ocean hadn't been discovered by Columbus.[2]

Historians, who were against Columbus, noted that, II Juan wanted to entrust Sanchez with discovering those lands as he was in the west after surviving in the catastrophe. Columbus rendered the navigator harmless as he had prepared his own project for the discovery of places located in the west of the Atlantic Ocean and didn't want any competitor in this work.

As I mentioned above, the Spanish monarchs had to keep promises if Columbus could discover coasts of the New World. People, who were close to the palace, were obliged to make up such events in order to disgrace the Genoese traveler, who was appointed admiral after the first travel. They even enlisted scientists and researchers for this job. But it is interesting that, this idea was supported by some scientists even after the struggle for inheritance ended.

This thought is so preconceived because when seamen of the wrecked vessel approached the coast, there were a lot of people besides Columbus and explanations

---

[2] Свет Я. М. Путешествие Христофора Колумба. М., 1956.

were made with participation of them. The Peruvian chronicler Garcilaso de la Vega, Francisco Lopez de Gomara and George Blon didn't want to deny services of Columbus when mentioned name of Huelva and noted that he had met the famous traveler. They only wanted to emphasize that, the Genoese seaman had got necessary information for realization of his transatlantic travel from Huelva. But as Christopher Columbus was very experienced navigator, he couldn't believe in such unserious, inexact information. He was sure that, America was far from Madeira Islands and it was impossible to reach there without knowing coordinates. Alonso de Huelva might meet with any island – even with Green Cape Islands.

This strange idea can't cast a shadow on the authority of Columbus. It was written in Garcilaso de la Vega's book that, Alonso Sanchez sailed in an unknown direction for 28-29 days under the influence of the hurricane and approached Santo Domingo Island. How it was possible? It means that, the vessel, which was pushed towards the west, met with Gulfstream current and could run away from it easily. It isn't convincing as in that case the Portuguese could discover unknown lands located in the west of the Atlantic Ocean before the first travel of Columbus. The Portuguese had sent there expeditions under the leadership of Vogado, Telles and Van Olmen, but none of those expeditions resulted in success.

Ambitions of Columbus and Vespucci's ruse

As it was mentioned above, coasts of the New World was named "America" after death of Columbus. Otherwise, the admiral could defend his rights. Vespucci used his rival's death for realization of his plans. The Florentine accountant knew that, Columbus wouldn't allow to name the continent he discovered, America if he was alive. Of course, rights of Columbus could be defended by the admiral's friends and colleagues too. But they participated in investigation of the New World within some expeditions and hadn't opportunity for returning to Spain during that period. In spite of it, scientists and seamen, who were in Spain, mentioned that, Vespucci was a conjurer, crafty person, profiteer and venturesome person. Because he tried to steal the success achieved by Columbus.

As it was noted in the historical sources, Columbus always praised the Florentine accountant, but he didn't justify admiral's confidence. It seems that, Amerigo Vespucci established relation with Columbus in order to learn secrets of the discovery of the coasts of the New World.

Some specialists may ask, how could Columbus declare himself discoverer of the New World, if he didn't know that discovered unknown lands when reached Guanahani Island of Bahamas? According to the most historical sources, the Genoese admiral thought that he had reached part of Asia during all of his travels. It could be understandable if Columbus sailed to the coasts of America once. But the admiral traveled there for four times and couldn't understand that he had reached the fourth continent.

I want to disprove it. The Genoese admiral found o lot of fresh water when entered the Gulf of Paria during his third travel (1498-1500) and thought that, it can be brought by long and rich river as in continents. Such river couldn't be in the island. It means that, Columbus was sure that he had approached the huge territory. He made following notes in his diary prepared during the travel: *"Is this a continent! Another world?"* He was almost sure that reached huge continent.

Conception of scepticism "questionable – R. D." was founded nearly in the middle of the 16th century. According to this conception, Columbus had certain information on existence of lands, which located in the west of the Atlantic Ocean and didn't belong to Asia, when he started his travel on August 3, 1492. Supporters of this conception were A. Vinio from America, Romulo D. Carbia from Argentine, M. André from France and R. Beliester Escalas from Spain in the 20th century.[1]

Columbus began to lose his fame after Vasco da Gama discovered seaway to India in 1498. Even he began to be called a conjurer and babbler. The Spanish Hidalgos in Hispaniola didn't obey admiral and his employees. There was a rebellion against him in the island and a lot of Hidalgos were killed at the result of the armed conflict. The island almost became graveyard of the Spanish Hidalgos.

---

[1] В. Л. Афанасьев. Текст воспроизведен по изданию: Бартоломе де Лас Касас. История Индии. Ленинград, «Наука», 1968. стр. 18.

Travelers, who returned to Spain early, informed monarchs about chaos, occurred in the coasts of the New World, and arbitrariness of Columbus by misrepresenting facts. It seems that, this process was the first stage of the plan on disgracing the admiral.

The Spanish monarchs cancelled monopoly of Columbus on the coasts of the New World when he was suppressing rebellion in the lands, he discovered. The Spanish officials cancelled the contract signed with the admiral on April 10, 1495 during his second travel (1493-1496). Some captains and navigators, who once were colleagues of Columbus, used this opportunity and began to organize expeditions towards the other side of the Atlantic Ocean as his rivals.

That decision resulted in losses for the creditors of Columbus too. Mostly his compatriots financed his travels. It is known that, the first travel of Columbus (1492-1493) was financed by Luis de Santángel – financial adviser and treasurer of the kingdom, who was close to the king Ferdinand, and Francesco Pinelli, who was known in Spain as Pinelo.

Pinelli was Luis de Santángel's colleague. Both of them managed treasury of the "Holy" Hermandad, who was considered police of Spain (he conducted law enforcement functions in the city and village communities of Spain).

The academician Charles Verlin wrote in his book **"Conquerors of America"**: "They agreed to allocate 1400000 maravedis for the travel of America. Other persons from Genoa, who were informed by Pinelli, allocated 150000 maravedis for Columbus. As Columbus needed 2000000 maravedis for his travel, he had to found 350000 maravedis in addition. That amount was given to the admiral by Santángel from the treasury of Aragon. The rich financers would get great profit at the result of the expedition according to the agreement between Columbus and them. Pinelli, who earned a lot of money after the expeditions, became one of the founders of the Chamber of Issues on India (*Casa de la Contratacion de las İndias)* in 1503".[1]

The second expedition of the admiral was financed by the owner of the trading house in Spain – Capetto (Juanoto or Cuanoto) Berardi, but he couldn't get a profit as died in 1495. Vespucci, who worked at the trading house after Berardi's death, paid salaries of seamen with

---

[1] Ч. Верлинден. Покорители Америки. Ростов-на-Дону, «Феникс», 1997. стр. 38.

10000 maravedis, he borrowed from the treasurer Francesco Pinelli in 1496.

Amerigo Vespucci partly financed the third travel of Christopher Columbus (1498-1500) afterwards.

In a word, financers aimed to get great profits from discovered lands. They also would lose monopoly on discovered lands.

The officials, who knew the admiral very well, Columbus was forbearing, courageous, fearless, ambitious and strong-willed person. As it wasn't easy to learn his secrets, they decided to crush him morally. That's why, he had to disgrace in Spain and even in the land he discovered.

Francisco de Bobadilla, who went to Hispaniola according to the special task in 1500, deprived Columbus of all authorities, arrested him together with his brothers Bartolomeu and Diego and sent them to Spain in handcuffs.

It was a great grief for the arrogant person and of course, he had to look for somebody to share his grief. So, Vespucci became the admiral's interlocutor.

There is no doubt that, Columbus had a lot of secrets on the discovery of the New World. Even the closest colleagues of the admiral didn't know those secrets. Too many people, especially officials, who were interested in the geographical discoveries, tried to learn those secrets. A dishonest person was needed for wining admiral's confidence and learning his secrets. It was expedient to look for such person among the compatriots of Christopher Columbus. Because he would trust them more easily. It seems that, Amerigo Vespucci complained about Spanish monarchs, mentioned that, Italians hadn't any perspective in Spain and he would move to Portugal. But Italians weren't respected in Portugal. Though he had discovered large coastline within the expedition of Alonso de Ojeda, monarchs didn't award him.

The admiral heard of Vespucci's decision, he had prepared to realize his desire to move to Portugal. Columbus shared information about lands he discovered around the Caribbean Sea with his compatriot and showed Juan de la Cosa's maps and Diego Chanca's diary in 1500. Though it is only my assumption, it sounds so convincing. Vespucci learned a lot about the territories around the Caribbean Sea after Columbus shared corresponding information with him.

Probably, the Florentine accountant approached his compatriot, who was in the desperate situation, as the spy of the authority. But Columbus didn't share everything he knew with Amerigo Vespucci. The Florentine accountant expected more suitable moment for it.

Thus, Vespucci complained about indifference in Castile and said to his "friend" that planned to move to Portugal. So, Columbus began to trust him. The admiral thought that their destines were alike as both of them had exposed to the indifference.

Afterwards Vespucci went to Portugal and tried to enter one of the expeditions, which would sail towards the southern continent. As it is known, he was member of the expeditions, which investigated Brazilian coasts in 1500-1501 and 1502-1503, and was able to misappropriate other persons' successes. It should be noted that, Amerigo Vespucci could participate in mentioned two expeditions owing to the information he got from Christopher Columbus. He informed the Portuguese about lands, which had been discovered by Columbus around the Caribbean Sea. That's why the Portuguese travelers refused to investigate lands, located above the northern coasts of Brazil.

Vespucci's manipulation skill

Everybody thought that Columbus lost all hopes. But Isabella of Castile allowed him to organize his next expedition as the proof of her respect to the admiral. That step of the queen enraged some persons and they used another plan in order to disgrace the foreign admiral.

As it is known, Columbus couldn't discover seaway to India during his fourth travel (1502-1504) and it roused the indignation of monarchs. Though he had discovered 2000 km coastline located on the western coast of the Caribbean See and spread important information about it during that travel.

Vespucci, who completed his mission in Portugal, returned to Spain as the "influential traveler" and restored his relation with Christopher Columbus, who had lost all authorities, according to the next instructions of his supporters.

The Genoese admiral had almost nothing at the end of 1504. But he hadn't lost his persistence and obstinacy. He tried to make monarchs to pay salaries of his colleagues, who had suffered with him in Jamaica. But he almost lost all his hopes after the death of Isabella of

Castile (November 26, 1504). Columbus needed his compatriots, as he was seeking consolation. Vespucci became more active during that period. There was a strange tandem between Christopher Columbus and Amerigo Vespucci.

Columbus was supported by Isabella of Castile when Vespucci's supporter was Ferdinand of Aragon. The supporter of Columbus died, but Vespucci began to be popular owing to his supporter. Though it wasn't easy to remove Columbus from the public arena completely. He had contract with the Spanish monarch and Ferdinand of Aragon couldn't deny it. That's why he supported Amerigo Vespucci in order to crush Christopher Columbus morally.

Vespucci met with Columbus on February 3, 1505 and the conversation between them was very interesting. Perhaps, discovery of the New World and other enigmatic issues were discussed during that conversation. It becomes obvious after reading Christopher Columbus letters.

Amerigo Vespucci's defenders mention that, he never betrayed Columbus and they were close friends. The Florentine accountant was able to win confidence of Columbus and Columbus wrote following sentences in his letter, written to his son Diego on February 5, 1505: *"I talked to Amerigo Vespucci, who was invited to the palace in order to discuss some issues on travels, two days ago. He will deliver this letter to you. He is very honest man and agreed to help me whenever I want. He also isn't very lucky as many of us.*

His job hasn't been appraised as necessary. He will go to the palace and try to achieve some good decisions for me. I don't know what he can do for me exactly as I'm here... But I know that he will do his best in order to help me... Think about it: what can he do for us? He will do his best with the greatest pleasure, but try not to let him to know details. I informed him about my works, including exclusive ones and share I could get for conducted works. Please, show this letter to the adelantado (Bartolomeu). Maybe, he can decide how Vespucci can help me".[1]

Everybody considered Vespucci honest man according to this letter. The letter proves that Columbus trusted the Florentine accountant. He even wrote that Vespucci would go to the palace and had close relations

---

[1] Лиелас А. Каравеллы выходят в океан. Пер. с латыш. Рига, «Лиесма», 1969. стр. 250.

with the Spanish monarchs. Columbus needed to meet with Ferdinand of Aragon very much. He was sure that Amerigo Vespucci was an honest man. It proves that, the accountant had won admiral's confidence. Besides, Vespucci made Columbus to believe that he would ask the king to receive him. How could Columbus believe such non-sense? How could Vespucci ask the king to receive Columbus though the king hated admiral? It proves that Columbus was in the desperate situation as believed that lie, because he knew that, people had to wait for months, even for years for meeting with the king.

Columbus shared all his secrets with Vespucci as believed that he would help him. It was culmination of their conversation. Vespucci could get all information he needed. This information included information on preparation of the first transatlantic map, the fact that the fourth continent wasn't part of Asia, but unknown land, the reason, why he kept this fact secret, secret map of discovered land and etc. At the result of it, Vespucci described discovered land, as the New World though didn't know anything about major geographical discoveries, unexpectedly Martin Waldsemuller demonstrated map of the fourth continent in Sen-Dye, the

Florentine accountant made up fake travels and introduced himself as the well-known admiral among the elite.

The Genoese seaman thought that, Vespucci would support him on all issues, especially for the struggle for his rights. He couldn't even imagine that, Vespucci would deny all his successes after his death and spread forged materials and letters full of nonsenses in order to name the New World *"America"*.

Probably, Columbus shared all his secrets on the coasts of the New World with Amerigo Vespucci as believed that he was honest. Why did the Genoese admiral trust the Florentine accountant? Because Vespucci had helped him before.

The last conversation between Columbus and Vespucci brought only trouble to the admiral. Because all his secrets were socialized by another person. However, in spite of it, he persisted in restoration of his rights and regularly sent letters to the king for this purpose. Of course, his letters weren't responded because Columbus required too great privileges. The king didn't even want to discuss this issue.

One of the enigmas was as following. Could Columbus really reach Malacca Peninsula of the

Southeastern Asia during his fourth travel as he wrote to Isabella of Castile? The king had doubts about it. Maybe, the admiral really discovered the strait on the way to Asia and investigated coasts of Malacca Peninsula.

Columbus had some supporters at the palace and he could meet with the king owing to those persons. The king wanted to end his doubts.

Ferdinand met the old traveler politely in May of 1505, but didn't promised him anything. However, Columbus obstinately required realization of all articles of the contract. The king mentioned that independent law-court had to analyze this issue. Nevertheless, Columbus didn't agree with the king and noted that, he didn't need proofs for restoration of his rights. He rejected real property in Spain and life pension, offered by the king instead of his privileges.

The king ordered special council to solve that problem, but the council didn't harry to make a certain decision...

After Columbus was sure that, his rights would never be restored, he asked Ferdinand to declare his son Diego heirs of his rights...

Ferdinand rejected this request too.[1]

Columbus shared his secret with Vespucci

As it was mentioned above, part of the capital, which was needed for the third travel of Columbus (1498-1500) was found by the Florentine accountant. Besides, he financed travels of the other Spanish expedition towards another side of the Atlantic Ocean. Perhaps, it was Alonso Ojeda's expedition and Vespucci participated at that travel as the financer.

Probably, *"Lost map of Columbus"*, which was considered greatest secret of the admiral, was also shown to Amerigo Vespucci by him. Christopher Columbus could discover coasts of the New World at the result of the first expedition towards another side of the Atlantic Ocean owing to that map.

Columbus planned to broaden his activity by researching the continent he discovered, during every travel. Perhaps, he would discover new territories if

---

[1] Лиелас А. Каравеллы выходят в океан. Пер. с латыш. Рига, «Лиесма», 1969. стр. 251.

could get opportunity to organize fifth travel to the coasts of the New World. Nevertheless, he and his children had rights on discovered lands. There was following note in the contract signed with the traveler: Columbus hadn't right of debate with Ferdinand of Aragon or Isabella of Castile for rights on mentioned lands as long as he lived. Because he had deceived the Spanish monarchs. It has been proved that, children of Columbus began to try to defend their rights after the death of the admiral. There were great court sessions on this issue in Spain.

A lot of facts began to be cleared up according to these explanations. It turns out that Columbus tried to deceive the world community, besides the Spanish monarchs. These facts helped his opponents to disgrace Columbus. I came to the following conclusion after analyzing documents on the activity of Columbus: He deceived the Spanish monarchs when signed the contract. Ferdinand of Aragon and Isabella of Castile couldn't understand ruse of the professional traveler. The Spanish monarchs thought that they deceived him when signed the contract and gave Columbus privileges he wanted. According to the conditions of the contract, Columbus would have rights on discovered lands and those rights would pass down from generation to generation. He would be admiral and vice-king of discovered lands after the discovery.

According to the history, Columbus went ashore together with the captain of the vessel *"Pinta"* Martin Alonso Pinson, captain of *"Ninia"* Vicente Janez Pinson, notary and inspector as soon as Guanahini was discovered and titles of Columbus were declared after the flag of Castile was sticked into the ground there. As it is known, Ferdinand of Aragon and Isabella of Castile kept their promises, but they knew that Columbus wouldn't get any rights on discovered lands actually, because the admiral had to reach Asia according to the project.

Christopher Columbus might reach Japan, Chine or India in the East Asia and they were powerful independent countries of Asia. He wouldn't be able to require rights on the territories of independent countries. The Spanish monarchs knew it very well and thought that they could deceive Columbus. Ferdinand of Aragon, who was considered prescient politician and skilful commander, gave Columbus fantastic privileges and wanted him to discover western way to Asia, which was very important for Spain, at his wife's urgent request. However, monarchs couldn't even imagine that, there was an unknown continent in the western hemisphere between Europe and Asia. They had reports of geographers, cartographers, astronomers, cosmographers and mathematicians, who worked for the University of Salamanca and other educational establishments, about linear measures of the Earth.

Actually, the king of Spain Ferdinand of Aragon was considered the most prescient politician of his time. He conducted all jobs cautiously and never made hasty steps. He tried not to make hasty steps about the contract signed with Columbus as well. But the traveler achieved his goal as Isabella of Castile approved his adherence to principles, resoluteness and optimism. The queen appraised skills and experience of Columbus and believed that he would achieve success. Ferdinand of Aragon accepted the traveler's conditions owing to the queen. But Columbus was deprived of his rights after his real purpose was found out.

The great mistake of the Spanish monarchs was made by accident. Contract was signed between them and Columbus in 1492. Nobody knew in 1492 that, there was a huge land area on the Atlantic Ocean, between Europe and Asia. That's why the king was deceived when he wanted to deceive the traveler. Afterwards Ferdinand noted that he believed that, the Earth was spherical, but couldn't imagine that it was larger than known. Because the king based on the reports of the Florentine scientist Paolo Toscanelli as he was considered the most talanted scientist. All leading scientists believed that the Earth was spherical when the map (the map, made by the scientist in 1474) appeared in Europe. They thought that there was only Asia on the other side of the Atlantic Ocean.

You may ask that, how I came to this conclusion.

Because all leading scientists of Europe imagined the Earth so. The Greek scientist Eratosthenes noted in the 3rd century that, if the Atlantic Ocean wasn't huge, it would be possible to sail to India from the Iberian Peninsula through the same parallel. Toscanelli and everybody thought so. Only Columbus knew that, there was unknown huge land on the other side of the Atlantic Ocean. But he described Asia on the other side of the Atlantic Ocean on his map.

It may be asked that, why researchers and travelers didn't use the material proving existence of the fourth continent if Columbus had it. I can mention some of them including Alonso Pinzón. I have a basis for it.

It is known that, Martin Alonso Pinzón conducted all tasks of the expedition leader till October 6 during the first travel of Columbus. But he began to display stubbornness after mentioned date. Perhaps, at first Pinzón was pleased because the expedition sailed through the west and he knew that route. Though Columbus kept real route of the travel secret, Pinzón almost knew real coordinates. The land wasn't seen though they had overcome about 4200 km according to his calculations. Martin Alonso also had made a diary on the travel as Columbus do. He knew that, they had overcome 4200 km according to his notes.

According to the historical sources, Martin Alonso started negotiations with the Genoese seaman on October 6 and required him to change direction towards the southwest. It was because Brazilian coasts were situated there.

An interesting event occurred in 1515: Heir of Columbus Diego Colón brought an action against the Spanish authority for his rights on the New World. Juan de Fonseca (he managed new lands discovered on the coasts of the New World), who was close to the king of Spain, prepared interrogation materials consisted of 24 paragraphs. It was noted on one of the paragraphs that, Columbus didn't play any role in discovery of new lands.

This job was conducted by Pedro Ruiz and he looked for witnesses in the cities of Andalusia.

Main function of Pedro Ruis included: he made witnesses to acknowledge that, another side of the Atlantic Ocean was discovered by the seamen of Castile before Columbus and the Genoese seaman registrated his discovery with their support.

The necessary answer was given by the son of Martin Alonso Pinzón – Arias Pérez. Pérez mentioned that, he was in Rome with his father in 1491 and found a material on unknown lands, which was prepared by the cosmographer and was kept in the library belonging to Pope. He said that his father sent that material to the admiral and Columbus changed direction of the expedition towards the southwest after receiving it.

Arias Pérez tried to convince people that, the expedition was managed by Alonso Pinzón according to the route described on the material found in the library of Pope, but not by Columbus.

I think Martin Alonso also had the map of the fourth continent as Columbus. It means that, there were several copies of such maps in the libraries of most cities located in the Apennine Peninsula, especially in Vatican or Rome.

Thus, Columbus changed direction of the expedition towards the southwest on October 7, but he didn't do it on the request of Martin Alonso. He did it owing to the birds flying towards that direction as he noted in his diary. Nevertheless, seamen rise in rebel on the request of Martin Alonso as they were dissatisfied of the long travel and required to return to Spain. Columbus asked them to wait for three days and discovered new continent on October 12. This fact was noted by the participant of the first travel of Juan Nino – Francesco Morales. He unmasked insidious purpose of Martin Alonso.[1]

There is no doubt that, opponents of Columbus will not agree with me. They may ask if Columbus was the most intelligent and well-informed person of his time. There isn't much information proving it in the historical sources. Most people didn't believe when I mentioned that, Columbus learned a lot about activity of the Greek scientist Eratosthenes.

Columbus read too many books when he was in Italy, Portugal and Spain. He read books of Strabo, Plutarch, Pliny the Elder, Aristotle, Sophocles, Tusi, Ibn Sina,

---

[1] R. Dəniz. Xristofor Kolumb, Nəsirəddin Tusi və Amerika qitəsinin həqiqi kəşfi. Bakı, 2014. Səh. 272-273.

Biruni and other scientists. Columbus went to the coasts of the New World basing on the measures determined by Eratosthenes and the structure of the Earth determined by Muhammad Nasiraddin Tusi. He learned a lot after reading mentioned books, but kept everything he learnt secret. But Vespucci was an exception as he had won admiral's confidence. The Florentine accountant could learn secrets of Columbus, who had exact information about existence of lands on the other side of the Atlantic Ocean. Besides, Vespucci could get some reports made during different travels.

It was really possible as Vespucci was a financer of the third expedition of Columbus in 1498 and was considered his nonofficial companion.

It was written in the book **"Hundred genius sea travelers"**: "Perhaps, the Genoese traveler didn't know that, his friend Vespucci was an active participant of the Spanish expeditions towards West India as the authoritative representative of Berardi's trading house in 1495 against the contract signed between Columbus and Spanish authority. Maybe, Columbus knew it and thought that, the reason of his failures wasn't financial operations of Berardi, but his influential enemies and policy of catholic kings. As Vespucci had allocated a lot of money for the expedition of Columbus, the trade house of Italy had to expect his success".[1]

Naming the forth continent America was a great injustice

One of the most important events happened at the beginning of the 16th century was naming the continent, discovered by Christopher Columbus on October 12, 1492, America. That name began to appear on the maps without consent of the most leading scientists. Nobody paid attention to this event though it was enough urgent at first. That territory began to be named America on 80 percent of maps made by European cartographers. The name *"America"* began to be serious problem after it was often seen on the maps. Discovered continent wasn't mentioned as America in Spain, Portugal and Italy and it was temporarily mentioned as the coasts of the New

[1] Авадяева Е. Н., Зданович Л. И. Сто великих море-плавателей. Москва, «Вече», 1999 г. стр. 75.

World in Europe. Most cartographers and geographers of the Pyreness Peninsula mentioned that, it was difficult for them to name the continent discovered by Columbus America. They named the new continent *"New World"* or *"Land of the Holy Cross"*. Some of them did it even after the name *"America"* appeared.

Though a lot of books and scientific articles have been written about Vespucci, there are still oppositions about his activity. Though the Florentine accountant has supporters, he has opponents at the same time. Why do such oppositions exist? Are there a lot of obscurities in the biography of Vespucci that cause to doubt his successes in major geographical discoveries? But one of the largest continents of the world has been named in honor of him?!

The Florentine accountant acquainted with the well-known sea traveler several years after he moved to Spain. But he hadn't participated in the travels towards the coasts of the New World organized by Columbus. In spite of it, Vespucci was aware of results of the admiral's travels. He created relations with geographers and cartographers and used their helps for realization of his plans.

Though investigation of western coasts of Africa by the Portuguese wasn't so important in Europe during the authority of the Prince Enrique, travels of Columbus, Bartolomeu Dias, Vasco da Gama and Pedro Cabral caused great resonance among scientists in the 90th years of the 15th century.

Why was that continent named *"America"* instead of *"Colombia"*? Everybody knows that, it was discovered by Columbus. Vespucci reached it seven years after the travel of the Genoese traveler. The specialists of this field had to prevent this injustice. The reason of this injustice was to name lands, located on the other side of the Atlantic Ocean, in honor of Vespucci, in order to steal fame of Columbus.

Cartographers and scientists created desperate situation for realistic persons by naming the new continent America. It would be just to name it Atlántida. Columbus had almost found Atlántida lost in the ancient times. Most scientists of the ancient times and Middle Ages thought that, Atlántida was situated in the western part of the Atlantic Ocean. At least, the northern continent could be named Colombia as Columbus had devoted most of his life to this discovery.

It should be noted that, other cartographers were more careful than Waldsemuller. There weren't the words "canal" and *"America"* on the map of the Holland Johan Roys (1508) and the southern continent was named *"Land of the Holy Cross or New World"*. The southern part of the continent was named *"Unknown land"* on the map of the Pole cartographer Jan Stobnicki, made in Krakow in 1512. This map was completely different from the map made by Waldsemuller. The name *"America"* wasn't used there. It isn't difficult to understand the reason. Some scientists didn't want to use Vespucci's name in order to prevent injustice.

It proves that, scientists and cartographers didn't agree with Waldsemuller's opinion. The doubts began to justify themselves. It seems that, the document, where the coasts of the New World, discovered by Columbus, were named America, was given to the German scientist by someone. Perhaps, Vespucci had an exceptional role in this process as it was advantageous for the Florentine accountant.

Unfortunately, the king of Spain Ferdinand of Aragon was jealous of the well-known sea traveler. Discovered continent could be named in honor of Columbus if he requested great privileges from the king. Vespucci could use this conflict very well.

After fraud of Amerigo Vespucci was exposed (30th years of the 16th century), geographers and cartographers go great opportunities to liquidate the historical injustice. Everybody could use these opportunities, including well-known cartographer Gerard Mercador. Unfortunately, he couldn't do it.

As I mentioned above, maps, made by Mercador in 1538 and 1541 (According to the map made in 1538, he had named the northern continent of the New World America) caused great injustice. But of course, the Flemish cartographer's purpose wasn't like that.

Gerard Mercador (1512-1594) (Kremer) was a Flemish cartographer and had been living in Netherlands and Germany (in Duysburg since 1552) for a long time. He knew almost nothing about processes going on in Spain and Portugal. Vespucci was known abroad owing to his "third" travel (1501-1502).

Some scientists, especially J. Margolis thought that, Waldsemuller's map stimulated heliocentric theory of the Pole scientist Nicolaus Copernicus. Such exact map, proving that the earth is spherical, was considered initial visual document. The real author of Waldsemuller's map was unknown, as the secret of lands described on the map made by the Turkish admiral Piri Reis in 1513.

In general, only three copies of Waldsemuller's map have remained till the present time. One of these copies was got from one of the German princes by the Library of Congress of the USA. That map was found from the prince's family castle 100 years ago. But the auction "Christies" began to look for the forth copy of mentioned map and it turned out that the valuable document was in unknown businessman's personal collection. Even the owner of the collection learned it from the newspaper. I didn't know the result of mentioned auction, but I know that, so many collectioners, universities and museums wanted to get the map.

If such historical material was got by universities and museums, they could create favorable ground for its investigation. But researches give no result when such important material is kept in personal collections.

The globes began to be created after maps of the coasts of the New World began to appear in the science centers of Europe in the second decade of the 16th century. Though the travel of Ferdinand Magellan took place in 1519-1522. In spite of it, most scientists tried to prove that the Earth was spherical and showed it on their globes.

I want to mention that, the talented mathematician and geographer of his time Johannes Schöner from Nurenberg (1477-1547) is known as the inventor of globes (Earth and Sky). His globes made in 1515, 1520, 1523 and 1533 were interesting for the scientists. Even Antarctica was described in his globe made in 1520 though that continent was discovered 300 years later. The scientist's globe made in 1523 wasn't known by the world community for a long time and only the examination conducted in 1927 proved that its author was Schöner.

The North America was described as part of Asia in the globe made by Schöner in 1533 (Weimar Globe) and lines of Antarctica was drawn on it.

Magellan Strait was described on the manuscript prepared by him in 1515 before its discovery. But it was on the 40th parallel, instead of 53th.

The canal between continents wasn't seen on the globe made in 1515. Parias (the territory, located in the north of Venezuela and Guiana), discovered during the third expedition of Columbus (1498-1500) in 1498 in the south of Anthill Islands, was described as a large island

and was named America. Japan, separated from the island with the strait, was described in the west of the great island. The state Brazil, located in the continent looking like the triangle, was separated from Antarctica with the strait.

Besides the globe, maps of lands named America began to appear. Number of such maps was increasing before the 20th century of the 16th century. The common feature of them was name of the southern continent. It was named America on those maps. The thoughts on the fact that, the territory located in the north of the Caribbean Sea was "new" and "unknown" and it was part of the continent, appeared after travels of the 10-20th years of the 16th century. The description of mentioned continent began to be created according to the real discoveries made during the travel of Giovanni da Verrazzano.[1]

It is already known that, the word *"America"* was used for the northern continent (North America) by the Flemish cartographer Gerard Mercador.

---

[1] И. П. Магидович, В. И. Магидович. Очерки по истории географических открытий, II том. Москва, "Просвещение", 1982. стр. 81.

He named the southern continent "southern part of America" and northern continent "northern part of America" on the map made in 1538. Afterwards the scientist decided to divide the word "America" into two parts and name the northern continent "Ame" and the southern continent "Rika" on his map made in 1541 as the territory, located on the other side of the Atlantic Ocean, was an indivisible continent. In spite of it, everybody named mentioned continent America.

The word *"America"* began to be used on all globes and maps after the second half of the 16th century, besides maps made by the Spanish scientists, according to the maps made by Mercador – so, fame of Vespucci spread in the world and Columbus began to be forgotten. But Spanish and Italian scientists continued to name the continent *"New World", "West India"* etc.

Of course, I didn't want to forget comparing opinions of other scientists and maps made by cartographers. There were real reactions against the injustice of the new name. J. Schöner accused Vespucci of forgery after 1515.

According to him, the Florentine accountant deceived most people. Besides, it was written by Bartolomé de las Casas in **"General history of India"**. Accusations against Vespucci were written openly. I agree with

Bartolomé de las Casas. Naming whole continent America is an injustice.

Some adventurous scientists deceived even their colleagues. This situation was created by Vespucci.

What is the reason of this conclusion? You may think that Vespucci had significant role in "enigmatic discovery" of America. Sharply criticizing his activity may be seen unjust. I have to explain my conclusions as there may be doubts.

Columbus died on May 20, 1506. Newly discovered continent was named a year after his death. Later this idea was supported by other geographers and cartographers. If Vespucci was an honest man, he could offer to name at least northern continent in honor of Columbus by saying the truth. He had to remember that once they were friends. He preferred to keep silence instead of to propagate the Genoese seaman's works and important discoveries.

Vespucci was an ambitious and envious person, who didn't appraise other person's works. He tried to show important results as his own successes. The Florentine accountant tried to misappropriate important results achieved by another sea traveler on Brazilian coasts and proved that he was an adventurer.

Of course, there are people, who don't agree with me. They may say that, he is one of the most important persons of the history. As if Vespucci proved that, the land, located on the other side of the Atlantic Ocean isn't Asia, but is an unknown land for the Old World. So, discovered land was named in his honor. I can't agree with this thought. The fact that, the southern continent was an unknown land was proved by Juan de la Cosa – participant of the second expedition of Columbus (1493-1496), but not Vespucci. I want to add that, the coasts of the New World were named America in the period, when Vespucci was a head navigator of Castile (1508-1512). It means that, his position and relations with cartographers and geographers helped him a lot.

The position of the head navigator was given to the person, who hadn't achieved any important success in travels

Following question appears when this issue is discusses: What had Vespucci done to gain the position of the head navigator of Castile? He didn't lead any expedition and didn't participate in important travels. Though the experienced traveler Juan Díaz de Solís, who was appointed the head navigator in 1512, and Sebastian Cabot, who was a head navigator in 1516, had led great navies traveled to the other side of the Atlantic Ocean. Juan Solís discovered Jucatan Peninsula and the coastline, located below it, together with Vicente Yanez Pinzon in 1508.

He was killed by indigenous Hindus near the outfall of Parana and Uruguay Rivers when discovered La Plata for the second time in 1516 (according to the experts of the history of geography, the Portuguese seamen Stephen Frosh and Juan de Lisboa reached La Plata in 1512 for the first time). They deserved mentioned position, but Vespucci's appointment was unexpected even for aristocrats, who were close to the palace.

What is the secret of it? Why was a merchant, who wasn't popular among sea travelers, able to hold such post? Could the Florentine accountant get that post by means of the bribe as he was an heir of Cuanoto Berardi after his death? We know that, Vespucci had left Spain for some unknown results and returned to Spain only in 1504. May be, the Florentine accountant was sent by the establishment of secret service with the special task and gained respect of the Spanish leaders.

When citizenship of Castile was given to Vespucci in 1505, there was such comment on the official document: *"For the services for Castile"*. It proves that, the king Ferdinand of Aragon was satisfied with services of Amerigo Vespucci and believed that, he would serve the state faithfully. What were those services? According to the historical documents, he never led any navy and hadn't great successes as Columbus.

Some specialists had doubts about the expression *"For the services for Castile"* used when citizenship of Castile was given to Vespucci. "In XIX this approach allowed Vespucci's opponents to accuse him. They said that, he had enter Portugal as the citizenship of Castile and sailed to Brazilian coasts as a spy".

Activity of Amerigo Vespucci during last two years is unknown. He sailed to the West India in one of the vessels of Spain as a captain or official or participated in preparation of three vessels in Seville for the next expedition, which was postponed later.[1]

---

[1] Авадяева Е. Н., Зданович Л. И. Сто великих мореплавателей. Москва, «Вече», 1999 г. стр. 76.

Vespucci declared that he had participated in two expeditions towards the South America and wrote it on his forged letters. I think his job was in ports of Portugal. There is no doubt that, Vespucci went to Lisbon as the authoritative representative of Berardi's trade center, but not as the cosmographer and cartographer and offered to finance one of expeditions. It seems that such proposal satisfied the king Manuel I and he agreed with some compromises. All events prove that he could be a financer of the expedition of Gonçalo Coelho, but not cosmographer, captain and navigator. That's why, Vespucci could get exact information on the activity of mentioned expedition.

He went to Lisbon with another purpose. My hypothe-sis is like that. The Spanish didn't want vessels of other countries to enter the Caribbean Sea when they discovered islands of this sea. Mentioned territory began to be controlled by the Spanish according to the Treaty of Tordesillas signed in 1494.

But the Spanish monarchs feared vessels of other countries, especially Portugal to enter the Caribbean Sea and fleece aborigines. The Spanish were sure that, the Portuguese entered restricted waters and conduct there illegal works. So, the Spanish spies went to the ports of

Portugal and tried to learn coasts, which the vessels, which sailed towards the New World, chose as the destination. But they needed to enter the staff of expedition and prepare report on the expedition in order to prevent doubts.

Vespucci could go to the other side of the Atlantic Ocean owing to his financial capital without any difficulties within Gonçalo Coelho's expedition. Though mentioned expedition couldn't reach restricted zone, he was sure that some vessels of the Portuguese sailed to thecoasts of the Caribbean Sea with the purpose of intelligence.

There was a rumor that, as if the Portugal sea travelers conducted investigation works in the north of the Caribbean Sea. There is an appendix of the land area above the left corner of Cantino's map. According to some researchers, mentioned territory is Florida, but others think that it is Yucatan Peninsula.

As it is known, Alberto Cantino lived in Lisbon when he made his well-known map in 1502 and got most information from the Portugal sea travelers. Though the Holland historian E. Roukema had mistakes in meridianal line in 1956, he noted that it was Yucatan Peninsula.

The historian, who analyzed names of areas on the maps, had come to the following conclusion: "A Portugal expedition met the northern coast of Yucatan Peninsula by accident when sailed to the west across Florida on 89 degrees longitude in April of perhaps 1503, then continued to sail towards the west and looked for the passage to the ocean (The Pacific Ocean – R. D.). The Portuguese went round the north-east appendix of the peninsula and sailed towards the south till they found Chetumal Bay without noticing Cozumel. Then they passed by Coral reefs around Tenerife, left Honduras in the south-east and reached the coast near Cape Camarón (16 degrees northern latitude) on June 18. They left the coast of the Central America in front of Cabo Gracias a Dios".[1]

The travel of the Portuguese towards the coasts of Honduras and Mexica at the beginning of the 16th century had important results and Cantino could prepare his well-known map almost owing to that unknown expedition. Did Vespucci play any role in gathering such important information? It seems that, he hadn't any

---

[1] И. П. Магидович, В. И. Магидович. Очерки по истории географических открытий, II том. Москва, "Просвещение", 1982. стр. 107.

difficulties in this job as a spy. Don't forget that, Vespucci had great capital and was able to be close to the influential persons, working at the nautical establishments, owing to it.

After gathering such important information, the king Ferdinand of Aragon ordered in 1512 to arrest the staff of unknown vessels, which tried to enter territories controlled by the Spanish. This order was first applied to the Portugal captain and sea traveler Stephen Frosh. Several other vessels of Portugal were also taken and so, travelers of other kingdoms didn't approach those coasts.

The Portugal organized secret travels to the Caribbean Sea and made maps of coastlines. They wanted to know towards which meridian did the lands, located on the western coasts of the Caribbean Sea extend as the Spanish kept those coordinates secret.

Vespucci met Columbus in 1504 after completion of his forged letters and learned his secret by consoling disgraced admiral. Perhaps, Columbus showed him the map of the forth continent and his notes made during the travels. But Vespucci showed those materials to the officials, who tried to disgrace Columbus. Vespucci was promoted owing to such services, which allowed him to win Ferdinand of Aragon's confidence.

What were functions of the head navigator of Castile? He had to test navigator candidates, give them diplomas for participation in serious travels and control preparation of globes and maps, get secret maps, made according to the materials, brought from the coasts of the New World, and keep them, give permissions to captains, etc.

Vespucci got this position in 1508 and the land, discovered by Columbus, began to be named in honor of the head navigator after it. Most travelers, expedition commanders, experienced captains and navigators of Spain began to be led by him. Geographers, cosmographers and cartographers had to ask Vespucci when they wanted to see maps and materials brought from the coasts of the New World. He gave secret materials to the cartographers and tried to prove that he discovered the continent for the first time. The scientists, who could get permission to look through important materials, had to spread this idea. All these processes were planned.

The Chamber of Issues on India (**Casa de la Contratacion de las Indias**) was founded according to the doctrine of January 20, 1503. The Chamber's functions included functions of the Trade Council and Hydrographic Office. Its purpose was to regulate trade relations in the territories, located on the coasts of the New World.

Geography and cosmography department was founded according to the decree of August 8, 1508. It is considered the first Hydrographic Office. One of its main functions was to organize drawing of lines of the New World and special council had to control this job. Merchants, ruined Hidalgos and adventurers didn't pay attention to the decrees and security measures and thronged to the New World with different interesting ways. Trade of maps was developed in almost all port cities and buyers preferred to buy new maps instead of old ones. As sea maps were too expensive and were tracked by the state officials, they were kept in the most secret places.

Authority of Spain ordered to make a standard map (**Padron Real**) in order to control mapping of new territories. A map had to be made under the leadership of the head navigator of Castile and control of the commission consisted of navigators. Members of the commission were well-known navigators

Juan Díaz de Solís and Vicente Yanez Pinzon and they were considered deputies of Vespucci. The standard map had to liquidate contradictions between cartographers, who made mistakes during the travel on West Sea (Atlantic Ocean), and navigators and create ground for creation of exact maps. Expeditions brought maps full of mistaken information and incorrect calculations. It was difficult to test them and to be sure that they were exact as mentioned materials were brought from suspicious places.

According to Veitia Linahen, official maps, made by the chamber, were kept in the trunk under two locks having two keys. One of the keys was kept by the head navigator and the second was kept by the head cosmographer. Sebastian Cabot – one of the foreign experts, who had worked for Spain, tried to learn secret of the mythical strait between England and Venice and favorites of the king of Spain Charles V were proud of knowing short way to Moluccas. After it, Charles V signed a decree prohibiting appointment of foreigners as a navigator or assistant navigator.

So, preparation of the standard map went on. Perhaps, it was a large-scale map prepared for the wall of the Alcazar of Seville. "All discovered lands and islands of India belonging to the authority of Spain" had to be described on the map. Every navigator, who sailed to the other side of the ocean, had to note every land, island, bay, port and other important elements on his map. Navigators had to present their maps to the head navigator as soon as they returned to Spain.

Navigators couldn't use non-official maps, otherwise they had to pay fine in the amount of 50 doubloons. Besides, employees of mentioned office had to control works of publishers, who published maps and sold them, and publishers had to have patience with monopoly in the map trade.

Control on the standard map was trusted to Amerigo's nephew Juan Vespucci and Juan Solis. They had to control prices of maps determined by the chamber. It proves that, Columbus and his colleagues might present the maps made on the coasts of the New World to the Chamber of Issues on India (**Casa de la Contratacion de las İndias**). So perhaps, Vespucci was aware of the maps made by his countryman.

Literature

Абрамсон, М. Л. Кириллова, А. А. Колесницкий Н. Ф. и др.; Под ред. Колесницкого Н. Ф. История средних веков: 2-е изд. испр. и доп. Москва, «Просвещение», 1986.

Авадяева Е. Н., Зданович Л. И. Сто великих мореплавателей. Москва, «Вече», 1999.

Андре М. Подлинное приключение Христофора Колумба. Пер. с фран. М-Л., Земля и фабрика, 1928.

Azərbaycan Beynəlxalq Universiteti. N. Tusinin 800 illik yubileyinə həsr edilmiş Respublika konfransının materialları. Bakı-2001.

Атлас истории географических открытий и исследований. М., «Главное управление геодезий и карт». 1959.

Афанасьев. В. Л. Текст воспроизведен по изданию: Бартоломе де Лас Касас. История Индии. Ленинград, «Наука», 1968.

Бейкер Дж. История географических открытий и исследований. Пер. с англ. М., «Иностранная литература», 1950.

Бейклесс Дж. Америка глазами первооткрывателей. Пер. с англ. М., «Прогресс», 1969.

Блон Жорж. Атлантический океан.

Верлинден Ч. Христофор Колумб, Эрнан Кортес. Ростов-на-Дону, «Феникс», 1997.

Вязов Е. И. Васко да Гама. М., «Географгиз», 1956.

Голант В. Я. Планету открывали сообща. М., «Наука», 1971.

Гуляев В. И. Доколумбовые плавания в Амерку: мифы и реальность. Москва, «Международные отношения», 1991.

Гумилевская М. А. Как открывали мир. Москва, «Д.Л.», 1997.

Дитмар А. Б. От Птолемея до Колумба. Москва. 1989.

Дитмар А. Б. Родосская параллель. Жизнь и деятельность Эратосфена. Москва, «Мысль», 1965.

Daniz R. Amerigo Vespucci, Martin Waldsemuller – secret bargain. "Lap Lambert Academic Publishing", Riga. 2019.

Daniz R. The scientist passed ahead of centuries – Nasiraddin Tusi. "Lap Lambert Academic Publishing", Riga. 2019.

Ионина Н. А. Автор-составитель. Сто великих чудес света. Москва, «Вече», 2000.

Исаченко А. А. Развитие географических идей. Москва, «Мысль», 1971.

Константинова Н. С. Путешествие в прошлое. Навигационная ошибка или секретная миссия? «Латинская Америка», № 5, М.2000, С.8.

Коротцев О. Как измеряли мир. Глобус. Ленинград, «Д.Л», 1980.

Купер Ф. Дж. Мерседес из Кастилии или путешествие в Катай. Одесса, «Маяк», 1985.

Лас Касас Б. История Индии. Пр. с исп. Ленинград, «Наука», 1968.

Ле Пти Фюте. Путеводитель «Бразилия». Москва 1997.

Лиелас А. Каравеллы выходят в океан. Пер. с латыш. Рига, «Лиесма», 1969.

Магидович И. П. Христофор Колумб. М., «Географгиз», 1956.

Магидович И. П. История открытия и исследования Северной Америки. Москва, «Географгиз», 1962.

Магидович И. П. История открытия и исследования Центральной Южной Америки. Москва, «Географгиз», 1965.

Магидович И. П., Магидович В. И. Очерки по истории географических открытий том I, Москва, «Просвещение», 1983.

Магидович И. П., Магидович В. И. Очерки по истории географических открытий том II,Москва, «Просвещение», 1983.

Марко Поло. Книга Марко Поло. Пер. старофранцузского текста. Москва, «Мысль», 1965.

Məmmədbəyli H. C. Mühəmməd Nəsirəddin Tusi. Bakı, "Gənclik", 1980.

Морисон С. Э. Христофор Колумб – мореплаватель. Пер. с англ. Москва, «Иностранная литература», 1958.

Муромов И. А. Сто великих путешественников. Москва, «Вече», 2000.

Письма Амриго Веспуччи. Перевод с латиньского и итал. «Издательство иностранной литературы». – В сб. Бригантина – 71. М., «Молодая гвардия», 1971.

Помбу (Роша-Помбу) Ж. Ф. История Бразилии. Пер. с порт. 7-е изд. М., «Издательство иностранной литературы». 1962.

Путешествия Христофора Колумба. Дневники, письма, документы, 4-е издание. М., «Географгиз», 1961.

Самин Д. К. Сто великих научных открытий. М, «Вече», 2002.

Самин Д. К. Сто великих ученых. Москва, «Вече», 2002.

Слёзкин Л. Ю. Земля Святого Креста. Открытие и завоевание Бразилии. М., «Наука». 1970.

Страбон. География. Пер. с гречес. Москва, «Наука», 1964.

Свет Я. М. Колумб. Москва, «Молодая гвардия», 1973.

Свет Я. М. Текст воспроизведен по изданию: Путешествия Христофора Колумба. Москва.

Свет Я. М. Севильская западня. (Тяжба о Колумбовом наследстве) Москва, «Молодая гвардия», 1969.

Стингл М. Индейцы без томагавков. Пер. с чешского В. А. Каменской и О. М. Малевича под редакцией Р. В. Кинжалова. Москва. «Прогресс», 1984.

Ханке Х. Люди, корабли, океаны. Москва, «Прогресс» 1984.

Харт Г. Венецианец Марко Поло. Пер. с англ. М., «ИЛ», 1956.

Хауз. Д. Гринвичское время и открытие долготы. Москва, «Мир», 1983.

Хенинг Р. Неведомые земли. Пер. с нем. М., 1963, т. IV, гл. 198.

Хепгуд Ч. Древние карты морских королей.

Христофор Колумб. Путешествие. Москва, 1952.

Шкловский В. Земли разведчик. М., «Молодая гвардия», 1966.

Цвейг С. Собрание сочинений в семи томах. Звездные часы человечества. III том. Москва, «Правда», 1963.

Ramiz Daniz

The plight of Columbus after
his travels

108 p.

Baku - 2022

Science-popular essays

Translator: - Hokume Hebibova
Computer operator: - Sinay Gasimova
Computer design: - Sevinj Akchurina

Printed in Great Britain
by Amazon